"Unlike other resources, time is irreplaceable. You can always hire more people, borrow more money... but you cannot substitute for time. There are only twenty-four hours in a day, and everyone... has those same twenty-four hours.

"Time, therefore, cannot be 'controlled'—at least not in the sense that tempers or expenditures or oil imports can be controlled. Then, what is time management?

"In a sense, it is a misnomer. For it is not time we manage but what we do with it. To 'manage time,' we have to learn to manage ourselves, our activities, and our relations with other persons. This is the challenge every manager faces—and the effective ones succeed."
—Myrna Lebov

Most executives today lack the time to keep up with even the new literature in their own field. How, then, can they find the time to read the avalanche of information on the latest management techniques?

The first in a new series of concise digests designed to present the essence of the best, most current and practical ideas in management technique in an easy-to-read form, PRACTICAL TOOLS & TECHNIQUES FOR MANAGING TIME deals with the number-one problem of all managers: time management or how to make limited time less hectic and more productive.

Complete with case histories, this succinct guide offers busy managers practical tools for solving time problems, including: how to define objectives; how

About the Author

Myrna Lebov is editor of business and legal publications for Executive Enterprises Publications Co., Inc. She has been managing editor of *Facts on File*, a weekly news digest, and is the author of two monographs on foreign and domestic subjects.

Practical Tools & Techniques for Managing Time

Practical Tools & Techniques for Managing Time

by Myrna Lebov

A HANDS-ON MANAGEMENT GUIDE

EXECUTIVE ENTERPRISES PUBLICATIONS CO., INC.
33 WEST 60TH ST., NEW YORK, N.Y. 10023
PRENTICE-HALL, INC.
ENGLEWOOD CLIFFS, New Jersey 07632

ISBN 0-917386-38-8 {EXEC. ENT.}
ISBN 0-13-694299-7 {PRENTICE-HALL}
ISBN 0-13-694281-4 {PRENTICE-HALL, PBK}
Library of Congress Catalogue Card No. 80-69133

INTRODUCTION
TO HANDS-ON
MANAGEMENT GUIDES

With this book, Executive Enterprises Publications Co., Inc., launches a new series of succinct digests of the best, most current, and most practical ideas in management.

The stress of unexpected daily crises, the too often neglected long-term planning, the crush of personnel problems, the avalanche of memos, proposals, and minutes from meetings are only some of the nerve-racking pressures besieging managers today. A critical factor in these ever-mounting demands on the manager's time is the enormous amount of required reading. The material may be vital for the organization's welfare, or essential for the manager's career development, but who has the time? In one survey of 500 chief executives, 415, or 83 percent, said they lacked the time to keep up even with reading in their own field. How, then, can they find the time to read the piles of books offering the newest insights into management techniques?

This series is designed to meet that vital need for information to help managers do their best job of managing. Each book will:

- Describe a management process step by step;
- Alert managers to the most frequent, and costly, problems;
- Offer practical suggestions on how to solve the problems;
- Define key terms;
- Digest key theories and ideas;
- Narrate case illustrations of problems and solutions;
- List a bibliography of major publications on the subject.

Book #1 deals with perhaps the number one problem facing all managers: time management, or making limited time more productive. The bibliography lists the books and articles from which this digest is drawn.

CONTENTS

INTRODUCTION

TIME. Most of us do not have enough hours in the day; yet others have time to kill. Time can fly, whizz by, march on, drag, or stand still. Or so it seems.

Peter Drucker calls time the "scarcest" and the "unique resource," R. Alec Mackenzie calls it the "critical resource," Alan Lakein the "basic resource." These three top management consultants clearly agree that time is *the most important* resource in the manager's life.

Unlike other resources, time is irreplaceable. You can always hire more people, borrow more money, substitute solar energy or gas or shale oil for dwindling and costly oil supplies. But you cannot substitute for time. There are only twenty-four hours in a day, and everyone—from assembly line worker to file clerk to corporation president to the president of the United States—has those same twenty-four hours.

Time, therefore, cannot be "controlled"—at least not in the sense that tempers or expenditures or oil imports can be controlled. Then, what *is* time management?

In a sense, it is a misnomer. For it is not time we manage but what we do with it. To "manage time," we have to learn to manage ourselves, our activities, and our relations with other persons. This is the challenge every manager faces—and the effective ones succeed.

PART 1: How to beat the clock

1. CLARIFY OBJECTIVES

Problem: Objective Confusion

For a year, Caroline Griffiths had been editor-in-chief of a practical law journal aimed at the layperson. Coming to the job after an eight-year stint at an erudite university law journal, she had brought to it an appreciation of the finer points not just of language but of legal complexities. Both the literary qualities and the sophistication of the journal had improved, she believed, since she had taken over from the previous editor, George Myers.

"I put in a sixty-hour week—and my editors almost that—but it's worth it," she told herself. "It's a better journal now, thoroughly professional. It deals with complex issues in a complex way. Myers made everything seem so simplistic." She paused, then asked under her breath, "But why are subscriptions down?"

*　　*　　*　　*　　*

Step 1: Clarify Objectives

Caroline Griffiths had lost sight of the *purpose* of her journal: to inform the readership in clear, lay, and easily understood terms about the legal issues that touched their daily lives. Her sixty-hour week, and the hours put in by her staff editors, did not contribute to the overall objective of the journal.

How to Define Objectives

1. *Define the primary purpose of your organization.* Does it perform a service? Does it sell a product? Does it aim at an elite market, a mass market? Your activities on the job should, in some way, ultimately help to advance the organization's primary purpose.

2. *Distinguish between long-term objectives and short-term goals.* Keep in mind what the organization wants to accomplish in the next few years—and the operational tactics adopted to achieve its aims. For example, a long-term objective of the United States is to become energy self-sufficient; a short-term goal is to conserve oil by lowering heating and air conditioning levels in buildings.

3. *Develop an overview of your responsibilities and your authority within the organization.* These duties advance the organization's primary purpose, which is *your* primary job objective.

Your tasks will be many, and will depend on your level of authority. For example, a line executive will be responsible for supervising the work of his or her department, as well as for maintaining ties with other departments—personnel, accounting, production, etc.—and for devising ways to improve the long-term capabilities of his or her unit. In contrast, the top manager of marketing, in addition to wide supervising authority and lateral contacts within and outside the organization, will also have a say in controlling and setting policy for the whole company.

Clarifying these objectives and obligations allows a manager to determine time needs.

4. *Periodically review your job content to assess changes in function and responsibilities*. A once-a-year review (at the least) can help you resist holding on to functions no longer relevant to your current job, and will enable you to keep abreast of new or revised goals adopted by your organization. You can then adjust your work schedule and priorities accordingly.

WARNING: After clarifying your objectives, use them as a constant guide in allocating your time. Don't banish them to a distant corner of your brain, or you will find yourself frittering away much of your time on activities that contribute little to your primary objectives.

2. KNOW HOW YOU SPEND YOUR TIME

Problem: Where Does All the Time Go?

Jack McGraw, office manager for the Handy Supermarkets chain, gathered up the papers strewn across his desk, stuffed them into a large manila folder, and put the package into his briefcase.

"Going to burn the midnight oil, Jack?" asked Tom Oakes, senior vice president of the company, as he passed by.

"Huh? Oh, yeah. I couldn't get to that office reorganization plan I'm trying to draw up. There just aren't enough hours in the day. I don't know *where* all my time goes."

*　　*　　*　　*　　*

Step 2: Know How You Spend Your Time

Jack McGraw illustrates a common problem facing managers. Beset by a host of time-consuming tasks and responsibilities during the workday, they work longer hours than any other nonfarm occupational group. Estimates are that managers spend between 43 and 47 hours a week in the office and possibly an additional 13 to 17 hours in paperwork and business reading at home, business entertaining, and commuting.

Hours Worked per Week by Occupational Group

Group	Hours
Managers, officials, proprietors	47.0
Crafts workers and foremen	40.9
Professional and technical	39.6
Operatives	39.6
Sales workers	36.6
Clerical workers	35.6
Laborers	34.4
Private household workers	22.2

Source: *Bureau of Labor Statistics*, Employment and Earnings, *Vol. 17, No. 11 (May 1971)*.

How to Examine Your Time Habits

1. *Keep a time log for one week.* Jot down the starting and stopping time of each activity. Memory is a notorious self-deceiver, so make your notes at the time of the activity. Include everything. Five-minute allotments spent buying coffee, sharpening pencils, chatting with Don Doe about Saturday's hockey game, or looking for a misplaced letter could add up to one of the hours that Jack McGraw spends, at home, on the office reorganization plan.

Be specific. With phone calls, for example, note who initiated the call, who the other party was, and what the call dealt with. Use a brief notation system. For instance, if you initiated the call, jot down "Me/T. Clark, stock inventory."

If possible, *ask your secretary to help* you log your activities.

2. *Analyze the time record.* Group your time outlays according to the activity and to the business function. Activities, for example, would include phone calls, meetings, correspondence, inspections, etc. Business functions would include customer relations, personnel, purchasing, etc.

At the end of each day, add up the time spent on each activity and each function. After a week, add up the total time expenditure for each.

What will the analysis show?

First, it will help pinpoint the most obvious time wasters. Does your socializing add up to more time than it should? Do you open your own mail, and are you disturbed by how much time it takes?

Second, the time log will point up the diverse, necessary demands on your time and reveal how little of it is what Peter Drucker calls "*discretionary time*," time that you can devote to the longer range goals that ultimately will contribute most to your organization—and to your career. Unfortunately, these are the more *deferrable* objectives, and are too often preempted by the crises that push to the head of your daily calendar. All the more reason why you must *plan* your time, and prune the unproductive time wasters.

Third, it will show whether you are spending too much time on functions of secondary importance. As management consultant Auren Uris asks, "Are your major time allocations going for top priority activities?"

WARNING: The log will give you only a silhouette of your time patterns. Don't expect all your time wasters to show up on it. You cannot, for example, log indecision.

---

3. SET PRIORITIES

Problem: Where to Begin?

"Am I ever swamped today!" exclaimed Bob Koren, sales manager for a large dress manufacturer, to his colleague Joan Cummings. "I hardly know where to begin. I've got to dictate some letters, go to the departmental review meeting, talk to John about his production unit's poor showing, talk to a fabrics supplier about slow deliveries, have lunch with Swenson, from advertising, and on top of it, I have a meeting with Jordan Brown."

"Brown?" asked Joan. "I thought he hasn't been buying from us in recent years."

"He hasn't," said Bob. "But you know how these things are. I agreed to see him today. For old time's sake. Oh, yes, one more thing: I have that year-end report to read."

*　*　*　*　*

Step 3: Set Priorities

Bob Koren's schedule is packed. But not all of the activities are equally important. Koren should set priorities, doing them in order of their importance at the time.

Assigning priorities will allow you to make sure that *the most important* activities get done; determine how much time each activity should receive; and reschedule in case a higher priority item develops into a crisis and temporarily bumps aside a lower priority task.

How to Establish Priorities

1. *Assign a value to an activity on the basis of its contribution to the organization's primary objective.* Time management consultants agree with their colleague Ross Webber that contribution to the organization is the *best* criterion for setting priorities. Allot the most time to those activities that will bring the greatest potential return to the organization.

2. *Differentiate between "important" and "urgent" activities.* "Important" activities are often preempted by "urgent" activities, and any system of setting priorities must consider both categories.

Edwin Bliss outlines five categories as a scale on which to evaluate activities and time use. They are:

- *Important and Urgent.* These tasks must be done immediately. For example, a report that the boss wants by 10 a.m. tomorrow automatically assumes top priority.
- *Important But Not Urgent.* These tasks may contribute the most to an organization or to an individual's career, but they are deferrable. Examples: taking an advanced course to upgrade professional skills, or developing a long-range marketing strategy.
- *Urgent But Not Important.* Clamoring for immediate

attention, these are the activities that, while not "important," consume so much of the manager's day. Examples: answering telephone calls, handling a recurrent crisis.

- *Busy work*. These activities are only marginally worth doing. They yield a sense of accomplishment only because *something* was done, not because something *important* was done. For example, a manager who has to make a difficult staffing decision may instead reorganize his bookshelves.

- *Wasted Time*. These are tasks for which Bliss adapts Ernest Hemingway's line that "Immoral is anything you feel bad after."

3. *Use the Pareto principle or the 80/20 rule*. The Pareto principle, named after a nineteenth-century Italian economist and sociologist, holds that the significant items in a group usually constitute only a few of the total items in the group. Although Pareto applied his principle to welfare distribution, modern time management consultants apply it to demands on time. It holds that in a group of items, 80 percent of the value cames from 20 percent of the items, while 20 percent of the value comes from 80 percent of the items.

Examples: In a group of ten tasks, two will produce 80 percent of the value. Or, 80 percent of the value is produced in the first 20 percent of time. Or, 80 percent of a firm's sales comes from 20 percent of its customers. Or, 80 percent of sick leave is used by 20 percent of employees.

The key to successfully applying the Pareto principle to time management is to find the tasks that yield 80 percent of the value, assign them top priority, and do them.

How to Apply Your Priorities

1. *Make a daily "To Do List" of tasks to be accomplished that day*. Number them in order of their *priority* and do them in that order. Otherwise, you may find that you've accomplished many

of the low-priority tasks, but left the highest priority ones un-done. The purpose is not to do the highest number of items but to do the most important ones, those that will produce the most consequential results.

Alan Lakein reports that the To Do List is by far the time management technique most used by successful people in business and government. Basically, it's a commonsense tool for setting priorities—every day.

2. *Decide what not to do.* Ask this question suggested by Peter Drucker: what will happen if this task does not get done? If the answer is "Nothing," don't do it, and use the freed time for more important items. Drucker believes that a quarter of the demands on the executive's time could easily be consigned to the wastepaper basket—and the organization would not suffer.

Lakein would undoubtedly agree. His pithy advice, "Work smarter, not harder," requires individuals to set priorities: those time demands at the bottom of the list get done last, and often not at all.

Many of those low-priority problems not "managed" will drift away on their own. So don't waste valuable time on them today when they may disappear tomorrow—without your help.

WARNING: Don't use long hours to avoid setting priorities. Consistently long workweeks are a liability—for both the manager and the organization. Studies have shown, R. Alec Mackenzie reports, that productivity declines sharply after eight hours of work. The habit of long hours may cause the manager to take longer than necessary to do a task. Instead of pushing to complete something in the office as quickly as possible, this type of manager will simply finish the work at home. Family life will suffer when the manager returns home every night with a bulging briefcase of must-do tasks—and a troubled family life generally will affect job performance. One study comparing successful and unsuccessful executives, Alan Lakein reports, indicated that many of those who ultimately failed had sacrificed their personal lives to their jobs.

Excessive overtime may well lead to intellectual and physical fatigue—and a less effective, less efficient manager. Health is also likely to suffer. Ulcers and heart trouble are two of the most common health problems associated with overwork.

The moral: strive for a healthy mix of work and leisure. Setting priorities will help ensure this balance.

4. DO ONE MAJOR THING AT A TIME

Problem: Second Things First?

"Leroy, this is Susan. Listen, where is that report on 'Sales Penetration of the Sun Belt?' My calendar says you and your staff were to hand it in by today."

"Well, your calendar is out of date, Susan," Leroy said with a laugh. "We're about half done."

"But Leroy, we need it. You're holding us up."

"Sorry, Susan. Last week, it looked like we'd finish on time. But then I got a brainstorm about how we could improve on our sales strategy in New England, so I shifted gears. I'll have the New England report in on Wednesday and then switch back to the Sun Belt. We should have that done by next Monday. Susan, you won't be sorry. We'll multiply our Massachusetts sales alone by . . ."

"Leroy, we were looking to the Southwest, not the Northeast. You're way off base—by a couple of thousand miles." With that, Susan slammed down the phone.

*   *   *   *   *

Step 4: Do One Major Thing at a Time— and Finish It

Leroy White might have had some brilliant ideas on how to improve sales in the New England region, but he committed a basic error in time management. His failure to follow through on the original project undoubtedly resulted in a substantial waste of time for him, his staff, and the organization.

How to Follow Through

1. *Stay on one project until you complete it.* This will save you time that would otherwise be lost in reorienting first to the new project, then back to the old one. Picking up lost threads can waste valuable hours.

Executives who do only one thing at a time, but many things sequentially, Drucker says, will expend much less total time than those who skip back and forth between many projects.

2. *Concentrate your time, effort, and resources.* Concentration is vital, Drucker notes, to cope with the multitude of tasks demanding your attention. R. Alec Mackenzie concurs: the ability "to persevere on a course without distraction or diversion" has enabled many an individual of moderate capabilities to accomplish more and greater things than an impatient genius who brings brilliant insights to many tasks, but completes none.

WARNING: People's most effective work habits differ. Some managers, Drucker allows, produce more by working on two tasks during the same period, thereby giving themselves a change of pace. But few, he cautions, can work on three tasks simultaneously—and produce superlative results.

---

5. SCHEDULE YOUR WORK

Problem: What's the Use of Planning?

Beverly Leeds had been named supervisor for a large cosmetics account at a New York City ad agency in January. By April, she was in a state of near panic.

"It's a madhouse," she complained to Meredith Singer, another account supervisor. "I've completely given up trying to plan my day. I always make an exact schedule, and it *never* works out the way it should. The week is never like the weekly plan, the day is never like the daily plan. So what's the use? I'm always exhausted at 2 p.m., when my most important and creatively demanding meetings are held. I function best first thing in the morning, but then I'm just looking over my mail or dictating some letters. I feel like I'm out of step with this job. Maybe I should give it up."

* * * * *

Step 5: Schedule Your Work

Having encountered some of the typical difficulties in maintaining a schedule, Beverly Leeds was thinking about changing her job, not her schedule.

But scheduling, as well as planning, is essential to managerial effectiveness—if it is done right. The following are easy and constructive guidelines to help you avoid some of the pitfalls of scheduling and make it a useful tool to serve you.

How to Schedule

1. *Make a weekly plan.* On Friday afternoons, list the tasks to be accomplished the following week. Don't forget to assign priorities to each.

2. *Make a daily schedule by transferring from the weekly plan, and the daily To Do List, the major tasks to be done that day.* Then add the routine tasks, such as telephone calls and correspondence.

Schedule the highest priority items early in the day. Then you won't spend the day worrying whether you will get to them. Draft that important sales report first. You can scan the daily newspaper later.

3. *Try to schedule tasks according to your personal energy cycle.* Everybody has high and low points during the day. Chart these over a few days to determine your personal cycle. Then schedule your most challenging tasks for your high-energy periods, your routine activities for the low-energy points.

Alan Lakein suggests scheduling according to "prime time." *Internal prime time*, he says, is the individual's best time of day to concentrate; it should be allocated to major projects requiring concentration and creativity. *External prime time*, on the other hand, is determined by outside factors. It is the best time to go after the external resources (usually people) you need for decisions and information. For example, salespersons will most likely be able to meet their customers during a 9-to-5 external prime-time period. Or, to use another example, if your boss spends her lunch hour at her desk, you might schedule time to meet with her then—and bring a sandwich.

Lakein notes that internal prime time for most business people is the early part of the day. This time, however, is often allotted to such tasks as answering mail. Reschedule this and similar routine tasks, he advises, to nonprime hours.

4. *Keep your schedule loose.* Don't pack every minute with scheduled activities. Inevitably you will be frustrated, because interruptions and emergencies will throw you off schedule.

Managers must be ready to juggle items on their schedule at a moment's notice. To allow for this, time consultant Merrill E. Douglass suggests a rule of thumb: save a quarter of your workday for the unexpected. Lakein cautions that you should set aside at least an hour a day for the unscheduled.

5. *Reserve large sections of time for those important tasks that require uninterrupted attention and contribute the most to the organization's primary objectives.* Consolidating discretionary time, i.e., time under your control, is, according to Drucker, *"the key to success for effective executives."*

The method you choose to do so will depend on the demands of your job. Some options suggested by Drucker:

- Work at home one day a week (an editor or researcher could opt for this approach);
- Schedule all operating work, such as meetings, reviews, phone calls, etc., for two full days a week and three half-days, reserving the mornings of those half-days for closed-door continuous time on major projects (a high-level executive might elect this method);
- Schedule a daily work period at home in the mornings (a possible route for the middle manager).

In order to free as much of your time as possible, simplify routine work. Try to consolidate similar routine tasks and complete them during the same block of time. For example, handle all correspondence during one time slot; do the same with your outgoing phone calls. (More about effective time management of communications will be found on pp. 44–46, 60, 62–65.)

6. *Review your schedule after a week or a month.* If you find that it bears little likeness to reality, or if you believe that you are ignoring your priorities, do another time log (see p. 15). Then revise your schedule.

WARNING: The higher up the executive, Drucker warns, the harder it is to block out uninterrupted periods of discretionary time, since so much time is needed to respond to the demands of people, crises, and new immediacies. Precisely because of the relentless pressures toward fragmentation, the manager must be ruthless in consolidating time.

Drucker issues an additional warning: don't fall into the trap of trying to make time for the important tasks by first clearing up the secondary matters. You may never get around to the major job.

The pitfall is that the most important objectives seem most deferrable: they lack the urgency of crisis. A *deferrable objective* is any project that will expand the organization in the long run but yields no, or few, immediate results. An example would be an organization's long-term growth strategy.

Managers at *all* levels require blocks of uninterrupted time to work toward deferrable objectives. According to one rough estimate cited by Ross Webber, the high-level executive may spend up to half of his or her time on deferrable objectives, middle managers up to 25 percent, and operating supervisors up to 10 percent.

6. DELEGATE

Problem: "I Can't Do Everything Myself"

Charlie Poletti, director of the Professional Recruiting Division for Hall & Co., an executive search firm, bit his lip as he cut through traffic on his way to the office on Monday morning. "Heavy schedule today," he said to himself. "In fact, it's an impossible schedule. Monday morning group planning session, interviews with three top job candidates, lunch with a big client, plus writing the weekly status report for the president. He'll be angry if I don't get the report done today, but I don't see how I can. I can't do everything myself."

*   *   *   *   *

Step 6: Delegate

Charlie couldn't do it himself—and didn't. Jill, his secretary, had typed the weekly status report for more than a year. She was very intelligent, eager to take on more responsibility, and, in fact, had helped Charlie compile the data for the reports. She could do it, he decided, with only minimal instruction from him.

Charlie's solution illustrates an appropriate use of delegation, one of the most important time management tools. *Delegation*, according to *Webster's*, "is the act of empowering [an individual] to act for another." R. Alec Mackenzie calls it "the essential tool" for executives to use to manage their time. Delegation of tasks to subordinates frees the manager to do the tasks that only he or she can perform.

How to Delegate

1. *Delegate responsibility for specific tasks or areas to subordinates*. To determine these, Drucker suggests that managers ask themselves: "Which of the activities on my time log could be done by somebody else just as well, if not better?" The purpose of delegation, he says, is not to slough your work off on someone else but to hand over responsibility for matters that do not need your personal attention, allowing you to devote more time to those that do.

Areas and tasks to delegate:

- Activities for which subordinates are better qualified;
- Routine tasks such as answering most mail, responding to periodic problems, and conducting routine meetings;
- Areas in which subordinates need training and development;
- Activities that offer variety and challenge to a subordinate.

Ross Webber advises managers to delegate activities intended to maintain stability and to retain those that involve change for the organization.

2. *Delegate decisions to the lowest level where they can be made intelligently.* Mackenzie counsels delegation down to the level where the relevant facts and required judgment are available.

3. *Clarify the degree of responsibility and authority that you delegate.* Six levels of delegated authority, each with varying consequences for the manager's time, have been cited by management analysts. (See table, page 31.)

Failure to clarify the extent of delegated responsibility, and authority to act, will create unrealistic expectations and frequent interruptions that waste your time and that of your subordinate. Set priorities and deadlines when you delegate tasks.

4. *Hire competent staff in whom you have confidence.*

5. *Discourage reverse delegation.* This is the process by which a subordinate shirks decisions or action by foisting responsibility for them on the manager. For the manager reverse delegation is a time-consuming dependence.

The most effective way to break this pattern is to refuse to decide for a subordinate. Instead, ask point-blank for his or her recommendation.

6. *Be prepared to accept differences between you and your subordinate.* If you aren't, your staff may be overcautious in assuming responsibility and pass the buck to you.

7. *Delegate as much as possible.* Most managers do not delegate enough.

Individuals who have been promoted often have the most trouble delegating. They tend to hold on to the operating functions they performed at the lower level. For example, an accountant promoted to accounting manager must learn to supervise and plan the work of others, not continue to balance the books himself.

Management consultants distinguish between managing and operating. Managing, says Mackenzie, involves "planning, organizing, staffing, directing, and controlling the activities of others" to achieve the organization's objectives. Operating in-

Delegation Patterns

The Manager Delegates a Task	and	Clarifies the Limits of Subordinate's Authority
1. Look into problem		Give me the facts and let me make the decision.
2. Look into problem		Suggest alternative actions, analyze pros and cons of each, and recommend one for my approval.
3. Look into problem		Tell me what you plan to do, but don't do it until I give the OK.
4. Look into problem		Tell me what you plan to do, and do it unless I tell you not to.
5. Take action		Tell me what you did.
6. Take action		No need to contact me further.

volves the actual doing of the business functions, such as production, marketing, etc.

The higher up the manager, the more time should be spent on managing, or delegating, and the less time on operating. Mackenzie and others have suggested that a chief executive devote 10 percent of his or her time to operating, 90 percent to managing; the top manager 30 percent to operating, 70 percent to managing; middle manager 50 percent for each; and first-line supervisor 70 percent to operating, 30 percent to managing.

WARNING: Delegation may take up more of your time initially, since you will have to train your subordinates and correct their errors made in the learning stage. But even if you could do a better, faster job on a *single* task, a *team* of qualified subordinates will eventually outperform you when *many* tasks are required.

Performance is the point. As Ross Webber points out, delegation saves time for the manager but not for the organization. "Delegation always uses more total time," he stresses; the intention is to free the manager to explore new ideas or procedures that will ultimately allow the organization to be more productive.

PART 2: Taming the time monsters

In the preceding section, we outlined a common-sense approach to time management, a general framework within which to analyze, plan, and organize your time needs and expenditures. But following those guidelines is not enough. Now we turn to the annoying—and destructive—time monsters that wreak havoc with the manager's limited hours.

We offer an arsenal of weapons with which to attack those hobgoblins that might be devouring your day.

CURB
INTERRUPTIONS

Problem: The Interrupted Day

"I don't know," complained Kurt Dellums, plant manager for the Rich Chocolate Co., "the day just flew by, and all I can show for it is a lot of interruptions." It was 6 p.m. and Dellums was riding down in the elevator with personnel director Jane Gold.

"We all have days like that," Jane consoled.

"But for me it's practically every day," Kurt said. "And there's nothing I can do about it. That new floor supervisor seems to pop into my office every ten minutes; Tom drops in for a chat whenever he passes my office; Mr. Gordon seems to be on a meeting binge—he's called three this week. And a nervous customer—not even one of our big customers—calls me twice a day to check on delivery of his Christmas shipment. That's my typical day! I ask you: when can I get time to really work? I've got to dig into that analysis of employee layoff costs involved in a switch to that new machinery, but with all these interruptions it looks like I'll never get the time to do it."

*   *   *   *   *

Solution: Curb Interruptions

The typical manager is plagued by interruptions. Sune Carlson's 1951 study of top management in Swedish corporations found that senior executives were interrupted on an average of every eight minutes throughout the workday.

As George J. Berkwitt wrote in *Dun's Review* in April 1969: "What gives the manager's job its nightmarish quality are the interruptions—the constant and seemingly endless telephone calls, sudden meetings and personnel problems that seem demonically designed to run his schedule off the track."

Interruptions are not always time monsters. A telephone call from a customer may bring an important order; a visit by a colleague may supply you with vital information; an emergency meeting may solve a problem that would have cost hundreds of lost staff hours in your department. The time spent responding to these interruptions contributes to the organization; therefore, they are not time wasters.

Many interruptions, however, *are* time wasters. These should, and can, be curbed. Kurt Dellums's day, for example, was consumed by interruptions that prevented him from working on his top-priority task of option analysis.

This chapter deals with three major sources of interruptions: meetings, drop-in visitors, and phone calls. But before considering these, consult your time log. That will pinpoint the interrupters, showing who they were and what they wanted. You may well find that the 80/20 rule applies: that 80 percent of the interruptions were caused by 20 percent of the people. Further, you may realize that many of the interruptions were unwarranted. If so, you can take action!

Drop-In Visitors

Managers need to know what is going on in the organization. Much of their information will come from visits by subordinates. Indeed, the Sune Carlson study on Swedish executives reported that chief executives spent an average of 3½ hours a day with visitors (mostly subordinates).

Many of the visits will waste the manager's time, conveying no really important or useful information. Since the manager does not know in advance which will be most useful, the goal is to *control* the number of visits, allowing the manager to focus on the job's major tasks, without closing the channels of communication.

In effect, the manager will be modifying the *"open-door policy,"* the original purpose of which was to make bosses available at all times to staff. Although increasing accessibility may be beneficial, it may also encourage overdependence by subordinates and invite an endless stream of unproductive interruptions.

HOW TO BLOCK DROP-IN VISITORS

1. *Close your door when you are working on a project requiring deep concentration.* Tell your secretary to disturb you only in case of an emergency. If you have no secretary, tell staff members that the closed door means: "No interruptions except for emergencies."

You might also work at home occasionally or find an unused office or room.

But don't abuse isolation. A manager *must* be adequately available to the staff.

2. *Require all visitors—even staff members—to see you by appointment.* Have your secretary screen and set up the appointments.

If you follow this method for discouraging spur-of-the-moment visits, make sure to establish *availability hours*—certain periods of the day or week when your staff may drop in without an appointment.

3. *Place your secretary's desk in a strategic spot so that all visitors must pass it before entering your office.* Your secretary will

then be able to intercept visitors who do not have an appoint ment and judge whether an interruption is warranted.

4. *Discuss with key staff members your plans to set up quiet blocks of time.* Ask for their suggestions about your new schedule, and tell them to keep you informed about any adjustment problems stemming from it. During the transition, you may modify it before you arrive at a "fit" amenable to you and your staff.

5. *Come to the office early.* Generally, the early birds are there to get a head start on their work—and to concentrate.

At the end of the day, in contrast, people are more likely to stop by to chat: they may want to unwind before facing traffic on the highway or the jostling of the crowded subway or commuter train. Shooting the breeze is a common way to do this, and it's fine—unless you're staying late specifically to catch up with, or get a head start on, a busy schedule.

HOW TO DISCOURAGE CONSTANT VISITORS

1. *Consult your time log to determine whether a few subordinates are constantly running in and out of your office.* If this is the case, ask yourself whether you need to delegate more authority, whether they are delegating their decisions to you, or whether their visits are a nervous pattern that needs to be broken.

2. *Set up specific times of the day when key subordinates who make frequent visits can see you.* For example, you might tell your assistant to see you at two or three set times, say at 10:00 and 2:00, when you can discuss all business. Only if a top-priority emergency develops should the staff member see you at other times.

3. *Ask the frequent visitors to group items that need to be discussed.* Go over several at once.

4. *Meet regularly with staff members to keep up on matters of mutual interest.* Perhaps you can arrange to have lunch with a different associate every day. Senator Charles Percy, when he

was president of Bell & Howell Company, found this to be an effective way to touch base with a wide number of subordinates.

WARNING: If your log shows that most of your interruptions come from new and different people, you cannot create blocks of uninterrupted time by talking to the key interrupters. Nevertheless, if your job requires a lot of thinking alone as well as a lot of public contact, you must create a system that will give you the necessary blocks of time.

HOW TO SHORTEN VISITS

1. *Go to the other person's office.* If a subordinate asks if he can drop in to discuss a matter, and it is not an emergency, answer that you will come by his office in ten or fifteen minutes. That way you can finish what you're working on, or at least reach a convenient stopping point. Equally important, it's easier to control the length of the visit when you are the visitor.

2. *Meet the visitor outside your office.* Or remain standing during the visit. The visitor will also stand, and the conversation won't last too long.

3. *Set a time limit at the beginning.* Tell the visitor how much time you can give to the visit; then have your secretary signal when the time is up.

4. *Establish a signal system with your secretary.* He or she can interrupt you with a call after ten minutes; you can say you'll return the "call" in five, ten, or fifteen minutes. The secretary will then "put through" another call at the time designated. With a clever secretary, many refinements can be worked out.

HOW TO CURB SOCIALIZING VISITS

If your time log shows many people dropping in for social chats that take too much of your time, you can:

1. *Place your desk so that you are not looking directly at the open door.* That way, people "just passing by" will not be able to catch your eye and invite themselves in for a few minutes.

2. *Say "no."* If someone drops by while you're trying to concentrate on something important, and asks, "Got a few minutes?", say "Sorry, no." Explain, briefly, that you have the billing revision report to finish and you'll have some free time once it's done.

3. *Resist the temptation to initiate frequent social chats.*

WARNING: Ross Webber cautions managers not to do away with all socializing on the job. Good relations with associates are essential; a judicious amount of socializing will keep those relations harmonious. Cutting off all nonbusiness conversations with associates will cut you off from them, and is sure to offend. It may also deprive you of information or gossip that you need to know.

Meetings

Peter Drucker takes a dim view of meetings, which he says are by definition "a concession to deficient organization. . . One either meets or one works. One cannot do both at the same time." Too many meetings, he continues, signify a poor structure of jobs: responsibility is diffused to too many people and information is not channeled to those who need it.

R. Alec Mackenzie reports that any group of managers in any country will cite meetings as one of their three most time-consuming activities. Participants in his time management seminars almost invariably say that "half their time spent in meetings is wasted." The problem, a friend pointed out wryly, was not knowing which half.

Despite their shortcomings, meetings can perform important functions. They coordinate activities, exchange information, build morale; and they can be effective in analyzing and solving problems and formulating decisions.

Ross Webber points out that the average individual is faster and more efficient than most groups, but the individual is likely to make more errors. When being correct is more important than speed, Webber suggests that groups, i.e., meetings, may be more efficient.

HOW TO MAKE MEETINGS COUNT

1. *Eliminate unnecessary meetings.* The first to go should be those called because a manager is afraid to make a decision individually.

2. *Prepare for meetings.* Insist that participants bring whatever information is required. Use an agenda that has been prepared and distributed ahead of time. Define the purpose of the meeting and know in advance what you want to emerge from it: a report, a presentation, decisions, etc.

3. *Set a time limit for meetings, making sure that you start and end on time.* Don't hold up a meeting for latecomers.

One way to make sure that meetings do not stretch on interminably is to call them for a half hour or hour before lunch or quitting time. Another tactic is not to allow the participants to get *too* comfortable. For example, try a stand-up meeting if you *intend* it to be short. Companies have found that stand-up meetings discourage an excess of detail and spur faster decisions.

4. *Restrict the meeting to those whose participation is necessary.* You may want to let minor participants come and go as their contribution is needed and finished.

5. *Impress the participants with the dollar value of the meeting.* Let them know the cost in terms of salaries, overhead, and time lost from major tasks.

Before scheduling the meeting, estimate its cost-to-benefit ratio; after the meeting, analyze the actual cost-to-benefit ratio. Keep the results in mind when you want to call the next meeting.

6. *Before adjourning, summarize the progress made or decisions reached.* Restate what assignments were given and to whom, and the deadlines. Concise minutes distributed soon after the meeting will underline its accomplishments, prevent misunderstandings, and save time in followup.

WARNING: If people in your organization spend a quarter of their time or more in meetings, check for time-wasting organizational structure.

Case Study: Toward Meaningful Meetings

Shirley Moran is managing editor for the school division of a major New York publisher. Promoted from senior editor of language arts books six months ago, she now manages a staff of ten full-time editors, plus a number of part-timers. Shirley has instituted a number of changes to cut down on time wasted at meetings.

Biweekly production meetings now take 1½ rather than three hours. To streamline the meetings, Shirley decreed that *only problem areas* were to be discussed; prior to that, *all* details for each project had been hashed over. During the meeting,

Shirley's assistant takes notes and afterwards distributes a one-page overview of all projects. These minutes inform everyone of the current status of projects and reduce Shirley's reporting time to her superiors.

Shirley has completely eliminated another meeting. Before she took over, all editors would fill out weekly status reports on their projects. The reports were handed in on Monday morning, photocopied, and distributed to the staff. On Tuesday morning, the managing editor would go over the reports in a meeting with all the editors and fill in gaps that she might have to explain when she attended the weekly Tuesday afternoon executive meeting.

The editors read their reports aloud. "Everybody knew it was a waste of time," Shirley recalls, "because we would just be going over what we'd already written and read. You'd go on automatic pilot as you'd read your report and sit through the other readings."

Shirley has eliminated the group meeting. Now, on Monday morning the editors write the status reports and hand them in. Shirley reviews them and questions the editors individually by phone. She then writes in the answers. The report is photocopied and distributed to everybody. Not only has the meeting between senior editors and the managing editor been abolished, but the Tuesday afternoon executive meeting has been shortened: because Shirley has obtained more precise information, the executives have fewer questions to ask her.

Telephone Calls

R. Alec Mackenzie reports that nine out of ten executives spend at least an hour a day on the telephone; four out of ten spend more than two hours a day.

How much time do *you* spend on the phone? Your time log should provide an answer—and analysis will indicate whether you use the phone in a time-thrifty manner. The phone can save time by eliminating meetings, trips, and letters.

Conference calls, for example, save the time required by multiple calls or bring together widely scattered people at far less cost and in far less time than do face-to-face meetings. Edwin Bliss calls the conference call the most underused time-saving device available to executives.

On the other hand, phone calls usually appear as one of the top three time wasters mentioned by any group of managers. Incoming calls, spaced at the haphazard will of the initiating parties, will fragment your concentration and derail your train of thought.

HOW TO MANAGE CALLS

1. *Rely on your secretary to screen the calls and reroute those that would be handled better by someone else in the organization.* If the call is about a routine matter—for example, a simple request for information—your secretary can deal with it alone.

If you don't have a secretary, route calls to other staff members yourself. Educate callers to phone subordinates instead of you. You might say: "Ronald handles that area. His extension is _____." Or you might say that Ronald will call the party back as soon as possible.

2. *Train your secretary to evaluate the urgency of the call.* If your secretary determines that you are the best person to handle the call, but it is not an emergency and you are busy with something else, he or she can arrange for you to call the party back. Some managers, in fact, work by an automatic *call-back system*. The secretary takes down the name and company of the caller, as well as the purpose of the call, and says that you will call back as soon as you are free. This allows *you* to control the phone calls according to your time needs.

If your secretary cannot determine whether the call warrants an interruption, a simple question may. Mackenzie advises a secretary in that situation to say: "He's busy now. Do you want me to interrupt him?" Most callers will not bear the onus for an interruption unless the call really is an emergency.

Time management consultants agree on the answer to the nagging question: should you answer your own phone and dial your own calls? "Not if you have a secretary," they say. Many executives, however, persist in "doing their own thing." Robert Townsend, formerly president of Avis, says that he dials his own long-distance calls. It's faster, and cheaper, than having his secretary do it, he maintains. Mackenzie vigorously disagrees. So does Merrill E. Douglass, who argues that the higher the person is in the organization, the greater the cost of time wasted answering and dialing phone calls oneself.

3. *Plan your outgoing calls*. Arrange to return or initiate calls at a time of day convenient for you. Rank the calls in priority order, then start at the top of the list. The grouping and call-back system increases efficiency by consolidating all your calls into specific periods and averting the distraction caused by constant incoming calls.

If your position allows it, establish certain periods of the day for receiving calls, say from 11 to 12 and 3 to 4. Inform your callers of this schedule, but add that it can be waived in case of emergency.

4. *Prepare for your calls*. Have the required information at hand, and know what you want to achieve: information, a customer order, a decision, etc. Then stick to the point. If you have several points to make, jot them down beforehand so you will not overlook anything.

5. *Keep your phone calls short*. Inform your caller of your time constraints at the beginning of the call. If you can spare only two or five minutes, say so; it will help keep the conversation to the point and allow you to end it gracefully.

Helen Reynolds and Mary E. Tramel, both consultants in time management and communications, suggest the following procedure to make routine phone calls brief:

1. Tell the person, in one sentence if possible, the purpose of the call.
2. Explain briefly.
3. Tell what you plan to do or what you want the other person to do.

For example:

    a. Diane, we need some more Executive Enterprises note pads.

    b. I just took the next-to-the-last one out of the supply closet.

    c. Would you please order some more today?

6. *Don't let the phone conversation drag on after it has accomplished its purpose.* Ending a call with a long-winded party requires tact, for you do not want to offend. You might say that you have another call or appointment or emergency. Or, you might follow the approach taken by one desperate executive who is reported to have hung up in the middle of a conversation—while *he* was talking. Of course, that tactic cannot be reused with the same party.

WARNING: To ensure that calls stay brief, keep socializing to a minimum. If you begin by asking about the other party's family, or weekend, etc., you are inviting a long conversation. Sometimes such socializing is necessary or useful or just plain enjoyable, fostering pleasant work relationships. However, constant phone socializing wastes too much valuable time—yours and the other party's.

REDUCE
RECURRING CRISES

Problem: "We Never Seem to Learn"

"Uh, oh, annual inventory time is coming up," Karen Loren, business manager of Grove's Department Store, said to Paula Leslie, the newly hired sales manager. "Believe me, it's tough. Everybody's running around, asking what we have on hand, arguing, saying the figures show we should have more of this, less of that. Or none at all. Everybody in the business office has to drop all their other work just to try to make sense out of the figures. We have to get it all done by this impossible deadline. And the hysteria! Wait. You'll see. And of course, once it's all over, we have to catch up with the work we let slide during Inventory Hysteria Week."

"I can't wait!" said Paula.

"You know what's so annoying?" asked Karen. "It's always the same. Every year. We never seem to learn. But I guess it's inevitable. Otherwise, it would have been smoothed out by now."

*   *   *   *   *

Solution: Reduce Recurring Crises to Routine

Crises come in two models: the unique and the recurring. Unique crises are often unavoidable, popping up because of a convergence of circumstances, personalities, and other factors. But many crises recur year after year, throwing the organization into predictable pandemonium, disrupting everyone's regular duties.

Recurring crises are a major, and unnecessary, waste of time. Drucker says flatly: "A crisis that recurs a second time is a crisis that must not occur again."

How to Eliminate Recurring Crises

1. *Analyze the crises*. Assess which are unique and which are recurring. Get as much data as possible and look for patterns. Armed with this information and analysis, you should be able to foresee recurring crises.

2. *Anticipate problems*. Eliminate factors that build up into the crisis. Draw up contingency plans.

3. *Develop new procedures to handle crises*. Drucker mentions one large company plagued by an annual crisis in early December. At the end of the second quarter, company management issued an interim report that predicted sales and profits for the whole year, although fourth-quarter sales were always low and difficult to predict. In the fourth quarter, middle management would fly into a panic; managers would drop their regular assignments as they struggled to make the actual fourth quarter figures meet the forecast. The solution: instead of predicting a specific year-end figure, top management switched to predicting a range that the company could easily meet and that did not require executives to waste time making the results fit the forecast.

4. *After a crisis occurs, streamline the relevant procedures to a routine that nonmanagerial employees can handle*. The simpler and

more logical the routine, the more people there will be capable of performing a task and the less time pressure put on the managerial personnel, leaving them free to resolve *new* problems. A *routine*, Drucker says, sets down systematically a procedure that the ablest staff members learned in resolving the previous crisis.

    5. *Don't procrastinate on important tasks.* What you let slide often builds up into the recurring crisis.

    6. *Get an early start on major projects, and set a realistic schedule.* Merrill E. Douglass offers a useful dictum: "Give yourself more time to do it right in the first place and you'll spend less time having to do it over."

WARNING: Save your crisis reactions for the real thing. Don't fly into a crisis mode of behavior for every problem. You'll wear out your staff's and your own capacity to give the extra effort required to resolve an actual crisis.

SET DEADLINES
TO HALT
WORK EXPANSION

Problem: Work Drags Out

It was Friday morning, and Gregory Kovacs, personnel manager for Merit Company, dreaded the upcoming workday. "If only Howard would . . ."—Kovacs shrugged off the thought. "Maybe today will be different," he told himself.

At three o'clock, he picked up the phone and dialed. "Howard, it's three o'clock. All the other department personnel reports are in. Where's yours?"

Kovacs listened a moment, then responded. "Howard, I know you *always* submit a very thorough and carefully written report. And it's very nice, but I've *told* you it's not really that necessary. I just need the information early enough so that I don't have to stay here 'til 7 o'clock putting the overall report together."

Kovacs listened again, then sighed, "O.K., Howard, just try to get it in as soon as possible."

He hung up, muttering, "Well, maybe he *will* get it in in 15 minutes. Miracles *do* happen."

*   *   *   *   *

Solution: Set Deadlines

Gregory Kovacs's dilemma illustrates the time management problems stemming from *Parkinson's Law*, which holds that "Work expands to fill the time available for its completion." Parkinson's Law can be the bane of any manager's existence, if he or she allows it to rule. But it need not—and should not. The key is to set *deadlines*, which R. Alec Mackenzie calls "mandatory" for time management.

How to Set Deadlines

1. *Set deadlines for each task.* It is up to the manager to determine time allotments and pass these decisions on to the staff.

2. *Impose deadlines for yourself as well as for your staff.* If the deadline is not inherent in the project—for example, you must deliver a speech to the stockholders' meeting at 2 o'clock on Wednesday—set one for yourself. Otherwise, Parkinson's Law may go into effect.

3. *In determining self-imposed due dates, weigh how much the task will contribute to the organization's objectives.* If required, more time should be allowed for tasks yielding the greatest contribution.

4. *Stick to the deadlines and require your subordinates to follow them.* For example, Gregory Kovacs should have laid down a set deadline for Howard, such as, "I want the department personnel report by 1 p.m. every Friday afternoon." Don't accept excuses for failure to meet the deadline, except for extraordinary circumstances.

5. *Make sure the deadline is reasonable.* An impossible due date will create tension and perhaps panic among staff. Overly tight deadlines can be met in an emergency, given proper motivation, but they must be the exception—or they will be counterproductive.

6. *Consult staff on time estimates before setting the due date*. A deadline set cooperatively, Mackenzie says, will generate commitment on the part of those who must meet it.

WARNING: Allow for the unexpected in establishing the deadline. Errors—your own and your staff's—and run-of-the-mill misfortune are always possible. Deadlines that discount this "contingency factor" are unrealistic.

BE REALISTIC
ABOUT PERFECTION

Problem: Perfection's Delay

The big sales strategy meeting was coming up next week, and Juliana Lopez, senior manager of sales coordination for Logan Design & Research, was to make the major presentation. She had been senior manager for only six months, and this was her big chance to prove how good she really was. "No room for mistakes," she warned herself. "You have to do an A-one job, right off the bat."

"But not to worry," she murmured as she emptied the contents of her desk drawer on top of the desk. She knew more or less what she planned to say. Maybe she had to refine the ideas a bit. She definitely had to talk to her five assistant managers to get all the facts and figures, and most certainly she'd have to polish the language. Maybe she should practice the delivery a few times—or maybe more.

"There's so much to do, I don't know where to begin," she thought. "But I have plenty of time. As soon as I finish fixing up this drawer, I can get started on the presentation."

*　*　*　*　*

Solution: Conquer Procrastination

Unfortunately, it was the third time that week that Lopez had rearranged the contents of her desk. Although she refused to acknowledge it, she was *procrastinating*, putting off doing a task.

Her story is a classic example of procrastination, a time-costly habit for too many managers. Mackenzie points out that managers who habitually procrastinate become interruption-prone and actually invite interruptions," making themselves susceptible to more meetings, more visitors, more phone calls, more paperwork, more office trivia.

People procrastinate over the important tasks. And people procrastinate because they consider these tasks either overwhelming or unpleasant, says Alan Lakein. To combat such procrastination, Lakein offers what he calls "the Swiss Cheese approach." The following are guidelines to this antiprocrastination method.

How to Overcome Procrastination by the "Swiss Cheese Approach"

1. *Identify the task before you as being top priority*. If you're doing a minor task instead of a top-priority one, acknowledge that you are simply procrastinating.

2. *Get started on the top-priority project by poking holes in it, turning it, Lakein says, into "Swiss Cheese."* These holes are "instant tasks," which require at most five minutes of your time. Thus, you can squeeze two instant tasks into the ten minutes you might otherwise kill before you leave for lunch or go to a meeting.

In attacking the project via the instant tasks, you should:

• Make a list of possible instant tasks;

- Establish priorities;
- Do the instant tasks identified as top priority.

For example, two of Juliana Lopez's instant tasks might have been to get a copy of the minutes of the last major sales strategy meeting and to set up an appointment with one of the assistant managers who could supply her with information.

Lakein sets only two requirements in compiling the list of instant tasks: you should be able to get started quickly and easily on them, and they should be connected to the top-priority project.

The Swiss Cheese approach enables you to get *started* on the project and allows you the gratification of completing a task connected to it. Fortified by this success, you are more likely to become *involved* with the main project. One, two, or ten instant tasks successfully completed often provide the momentum for you to launch your major assault on the project—and stay with it until you finish.

You may find that your major problem was simply that you magnified the project out of all proportion: by breaking down the project into human-size bites, you may discover that the project was neither so difficult nor so overwhelming as you had feared.

WARNING: Start the instant tasks as early as possible. Otherwise, you may find yourself working on them just as the deadline passes for completion of the whole project.

Solution: Don't Let Perfectionism Paralyze You

Juliana Lopez's procrastination stemmed in part from perfectionistic demands on herself. She wanted to make a no-fault sales presentation. The result: she was too intimidated even to *begin* work on such an overwhelming task.

Her behavior illustrates that sometimes the conscientious desire to do a good job expands into a neurotic need to do a perfect job.

Webster's defines *perfectionism* as "a disposition to regard anything short of perfection as unacceptable." It is a luxury most organizations cannot afford.

How to Overcome Perfectionism

1. *Aim at doing your best, but don't demand perfection of yourself or your subordinates.* Perfectionistic demands will create tension and frayed nerves without necessarily contributing to the organization's main objectives.

2. *Don't fear failure.* Use mistakes as a learning tool. Organizations must take risks to grow, and these risks court the danger of error. By making mistakes, Mackenzie says, you can learn something worthwhile; such lessons pave the way to bigger successes.

3. *Use the 80/20 rule (see p. 19) to curb perfectionistic tendencies.* That rule suggests that 80 percent of the value is often achieved during the first 20 percent of your time on a particular task. The corollary: perfectionism may translate into working too hard for only minimum value.

Solution: Don't Delay Decisions

Indecision is dangerous to the health of your organization.

One of the worst consequences of perfectionism and procrastination is indecision. And indecision can be fatal. It can immobilize you—and your organization. Mackenzie says that postponing a decision may be the worst possible alternative for a manager: the best decision made too late is useless.

How to Speed Decision Making

1. *Don't become compulsive about getting all the facts.* Set priorities on which facts are most relevant to the decision. Again, the Pareto principle applies: if 20 percent of the facts are vital to 80 percent of the outcome, waiting until you have all the facts may be procrastination—and a costly waste of time.

2. *If fear of making a mistake is the source of indecision, ask yourself what the consequences of a mistake might be.* Realism is important here: a mistake is rarely an unmitigated disaster, either to the organization or to you personally.

3. *Think about what you can do to minimize the consequences of a mistake.* Then make a decision and move forcefully to implement it. If you don't, you will have made the biggest mistake of all.

PRUNE
TRIVIAL TASKS

Problem: No Time Except for the Trivial

Ed DeVoe, executive vice president of Fun-E Toys, smiled as he completed the last sentence of the company's newest directive on travel allowances.

"Well," he thought to himself, "that's done!"

He got up from his desk and walked out of the office. June, his secretary, was not at her desk.

"I want a copy of this before she types it," he reflected. "Just so it doesn't get lost among all the other things on her desk. A walk will do me good."

DeVoe walked down the hallway, nodding to Mary Grimaldi as he passed.

"Don't ask," Ed said to Mary. "I have to go over Jim's and Kathy's New Products Development Report and put on the finishing touches. I just haven't had time to do it yet. I'll get it to you for your O.K. as soon as possible."

"Sure, Ed, but try to hurry. Mr. Donne was asking for it today, and I said you and your staff were nearly finished.

"That might be a bit optimistic, Mary. But we'll plug away."

Mary veered off into her office as Ed continued to the photocopier. A worrisome thought gnawed at the satisfaction he felt in completing the memo. "Face it," he told himself, "you're not getting paid to issue a minor directive on travel allowances. You're paid to run the New Products Development Department."

* * * * *

Solution: Prune Trivial and Routine Tasks

Many managers complain of wasting time on trivial or routine tasks. However, performing these tasks may serve several purposes, none of which adds to effectiveness as a manager. The purposes include: procrastination, satisfaction that something *tangible* is being accomplished, and ego inflation because only *you* can do the job well.

Ross Webber speculates that some managers may seek out detail work and trivial tasks because the "*real* challenges of managing are so difficult and anxiety provoking." (Emphasis added.)

How to Curb Trivial and Routine Tasks

1. *Consider your objectives.* If the trivial and routine tasks add nothing to your effectiveness as a manager, don't do them. Lakein's dictum makes sense: "Work smarter, not harder."

2. *Review the routine tasks.* Ask yourself what would happen if they were not done. If the answer is nothing, get rid of them. For example, Ed DeVoe's handwritten travel directive did not need to be photocopied.

3. *Delegate tasks that can be done just as easily, and well, by others.* DeVoe could have asked a subordinate to write a simple memo on travel allowances.

4. *Hire competent support staff*. You will be able to trust them with a wide range of tasks, from the routine to the challenging.

5. *Do routine tasks after the important ones*. For instance, Ed DeVoe's number one priority was to see that the New Products Development Report was developed and handed in by his staff.

Don't waste time on routine work and think that when it is finished you can tackle the big projects. You can *always* find more routine work to take up your time.

6. *Don't do your own typing, filing, or other clerical work if you have a secretary*. Time management experts advise managers not to write letters by hand. Instead, either dictate them directly to your secretary or use dictating equipment. Most prefer using dictating equipment: it saves your time and your secretary's. You can speak much faster than your secretary can take shorthand, and your secretary need not waste time waiting while you compose the material.

PARE
THE PAPERWORK

Problem: The Paperwork Jungle

"Dan, do you have that estimate that ABC Corporation sent you two weeks ago?" asked Melvin Warren, president of Warren Furniture Manufacturers.

"Sure, Mel, it's right here on my desk. Thought I might be needing it soon."

Schmidt started riffling through the piles of papers covering the top of his large desk. Two minutes later he was still looking.

Warren snapped, "Look, Dan, I don't have time to wait around. Ask Felipe to help you find it in that, that paperwork jungle, and get back to me on it."

He turned to walk out of Dan's office, then paused. "You might also ask Felipe to help you organize your desk and your files. I bet it would save hours· of time—yours and the company's."

*　*　*　*　*

Solution: Clear the Clutter

Managers who get snowed under by an avalanche of ,paperwork waste hours trying to retrieve needed, but buried, information. While some individuals claim a psychological need for the ferment suggested by a paper-strewn desktop, in most cases clutter impedes concentration on a single task. The eye is constantly diverted to yet another project or proposal or memo or . . .

Clearing the clutter means getting organized. It involves establishing a convenient work area and an efficient correspondence and filing system. And most important, it means not inviting or accumulating reams of paperwork—yours or your associates'.

How to Organize Your Paperwork

1. *Resist the temptation to pile papers—memos, correspondence, notes, proposals, etc.—on your desk.* Instead, devise an efficient filing system, with a secretary's help if possible, where you and your secretary can retrieve information immediately.

2. *Train your staff not to leave things on your desk.* One manager laid down a flat rule: "Leave reports or memos or anything else with my secretary, and tell her if it's urgent. Nothing should just be dropped on my desk."

3. *Handle each piece of paper only once.* Respond immediately, if possible, or take some action to move it along, Alan Lakein advises. This policy eliminates time-consuming paper shuffling.

4. *Write brief replies on incoming letters or memos, photocopy for your files, then return it to the original sender, with copies to go to other people who need the information or must act on the matter.*

When a formal reply is required, resist the compulsion to do multiple revisions. Weigh how significant the change really is, and how much it will contribute ultimately to the organization's objectives. With most but not all correspondence, a simple write-in correction would save your secretary time in retyping it and you time in rereading it and would not be a catastrophe. REMEMBER: perfectionism costs time—and generally gives poor value in return.

5. *For routine correspondence, use form letters.* For non-routine correspondence, use a dictating machine. Strive for a finished product on the first dictation try. Make the replies short. Lakein reports one executive's time-saver: he dictates only key ideas, then allows his trusted secretary to compose the actual letter or memo.

6. *Don't overuse the memo, a prime culprit in the paperwork bottleneck in most organizations.* Besides clogging the information channels, the memo can waste time and effort. First it must be composed, then perhaps dictated and typed, then transmitted, read, and disposed of. On top of that, you must wait for a response. In contrast, you can obtain an immediate reaction through a phone call or in a person-to-person meeting. Because of these drawbacks, Mackenzie advises the executive to use the memo as seldom as possible—only to remind, clarify, and confirm. The memo may be more effective, Mackenzie concedes, if the recipient needs it as a constant reminder; and it can save wasted telephoning time if sent to hard-to-locate people.

Edwin Bliss adds one more function to the memo's possibilities—to announce. Nevertheless, he counsels executives not to write when they can phone.

One other use for the memo: to spell out a complex problem or need. It can clarify the *manager's views* and avoid misunderstanding among recipients.

7. *Encourage your staff to include a recommendation in any memo that discusses a problem.* This will force them to think about a solution, not simply delegate responsibility for it up to you.

8. *Ask colleagues not to send you FYI copies of letters or memos unless they contain information relevant to your area of responsibility.*

9. *Examine last month's crop of incoming and outgoing memos.* Were they all necessary? Could they have been shorter? Correct your own time-consuming memo habits—and ask your subordinates to correct theirs. Not only should they not waste their time on overlong or unnecessary memos, but they should not waste your time by expecting you to read them.

10. *Have your mail and memos screened and sorted.* Tell your secretary to reroute or throw out material that does not require your attention. Give him or her clear guidelines on how to do this.

There are many possible systems to cope with paperwork flow. Devise one that suits *your* needs. For example:

One manager says that her secretary puts the mail in three colored folders, marked SIGN, ACTION, and INFORMATION. Another has his secretary sort material in ACTION, INFORMATION, and DEFERRED folders. The ACTION folder gets top priority, the INFORMATION folder material gets read on the train to and from the office, and the DEFERRED material is relegated to his spare moments.

Edwin Bliss recommends a particularly handy system for retrieving things on specific dates: use an accordion file with a pocket for each day of the month and pockets for each subsequent month. Documents—memos, letters, expected replies, suggestions, etc.—can be filed in the pocket under the day when further action is required. File folders can be set up in the same way, but the accordion file offers the advantage of compactness.

11. *If you sort the mail yourself, arrange it in priority order, handling the most important first.* Throw away as much as you can. If you can't get through the low-priority mail during the day, put it into a DEFERRED folder, reaching into it as you get a spare moment. Periodically schedule time to go through the DEFERRED folder. With hindsight, you'll discover that much of the DEFERRED material was unimportant, and you can easily consign it to the wastepaper basket.

12. *Encourage the use of a uniform filing system throughout the office.* Thus, if a manager, secretary, or assistant is temporarily away from the office, or is no longer in the department, someone else can find the information quickly and easily. Delegate responsibility for establishing the filing system to someone trained in the task: usually a secretary. See that a guide sheet, and perhaps a diagram, are drafted to help newcomers understand the system.

13. *Periodically weed out dated, unimportant, and unused material in the files.* Experts in record retention say that no more than one year of correspondence should be kept in the current operations files. Office operations personnel, Mackenzie reports, have estimated that 80 to 90 percent of paperwork in the files is never referred to again; some estimates are even higher. Before discarding personnel records, however, consult federal and state EEO record-keeping requirements.

WARNING: Managers should weigh the usefulness of these suggestions to prune paperwork for their own situation, taking into account such factors as the structure of their organization, personalities and capabilities of their staff, the manager's own communication strengths and weaknesses, etc. For example, while most time management experts warn of the time-wasting, paper-clogging dangers of the memo, some managers may agree with Ross Webber that written communications are more efficient than verbal ones.

VALUE YOUR STAFF'S TIME

Problem: Minutes Into Hours

Vincent Cutler picked up his phone and dialed Anna Gruen, one of the members of his staff helping to devise new office forms. Worried that she might be having trouble, he wanted to discuss the project with her.

"Anna, would you come into my office now? It'll only take a couple of minutes."

Anna hung up the phone and grimaced.

"A few minutes, huh?" she muttered. "I just saw him about the project this morning, and his few minutes turned into a half hour. He's driving me crazy!"

* * * * *

Solution: Value Your Subordinates' Time

Cutler's motives were good. He wanted to keep Gruen on track with the project and use his experience to help her iron out actual and potential knots.

But he was wasting Gruen's time. She needed blocks of uninterrupted time to devise the new forms. Moreover, she needed the chance to work the problems out herself, to gain the experience that would make her an even more valuable and creative member of his staff.

Although Cutler was sensitive to the operational difficulties in Gruen's project, he failed to see himself as one of her most serious problems.

How to Manage Your Subordinates' Time

1. *Periodically ask each member of your staff a question suggested by Peter Drucker: "What do I do that wastes your time without contributing to your effectiveness?"* Listen carefully to the response and discuss with the employee.

2. *Give clear instructions.* Tell the subordinate exactly what the assignment is, the extent of responsibility and authority being delegated, and the deadline for completing the task. Get feedback from the employee on the assignment, priority, and deadline. Be ready to compromise where reasonable and feasible.

3. *Don't keep your subordinates waiting unnecessarily.* Your staff members' time is valuable, too. If you are late for an appointment with them, you are wasting their time—and the organization's.

4. *Don't inflict constant interruptions on your subordinates' work.* Given proper instructions, the competent staff member should be able to do the assigned tasks without your constant checking. This is especially true if the project needs prolonged periods of careful thought and concentration. Of course, if the employee is not competent to do the work, you must reevaluate the wisdom of keeping him or her on staff.

5. *It is extremely important not to waste your secretary's time.*

He or she may be pivotal in organizing your office and your daily schedule, as well as in buffering you from unwarranted interruptions. Since the secretary's time is valuable, keep your interruptions to a minimum.

6. *Every six or 12 months ask your subordinates to keep a time log for a week (see p. 15).* Discuss the results with each employee. It might point out time-wasting habits—and it might also pinpoint *you* as a contributor to the time waste.

WARNING: When asking employees to keep a time log, don't imply that you are checking up on them. Such an impression would create bitter resentment and insecurity. Stress how the log can help them manage their time and help you reallocate priorities.

ENCOURAGE YOUR SUPERIOR TO HONOR YOUR TIME

Problem: Drop Everything

"Andy," Malcolm Sloane began, "hold everything. I need a comprehensive accounting report to present to our stockholders' meeting next week."

Accounting manager Andy Winnick frowned. "What about the priority tax analysis you asked for last Monday? That's what my staff is working on."

"Sorry, it'll have to go on the back burner. I need the accounting report by this Friday, so I can look it over before the meeting next week. You can always catch up with the tax analysis."

*   *   *   *   *

Solution: Encourage Your Superior to Honor Your Time

You are the one who must set priorities to determine what gets done and how quickly. One of the thorniest problems for a middle manager is a boss who is careless about time. What can you do if your superior wastes your time—by interruptions, unclear instructions, suffocating supervision, etc.? What can you do if, like Andy Winnick's, your boss is prone to dropping a rush job on you that bumps aside a priority project assigned a couple of days before. We will point out some general principles, then examine the particular case of handling a rush project.

How to Deal With Your Boss's Demands on Your Time

1. *Seek out opportunities to discuss with your superior the problems stemming from his or her time habits*. In most cases, a diplomatic discussion will pay off. After all, if you can suggest a way to improve your performance—and that of your staff—you will generally find an interested, and cooperative, boss.

2. *Discuss with your superior the time management techniques you have adopted with your subordinates—such as reducing interruptions, asking how you waste their time, etc.—and the results*. Be concrete about the payoff. For example, if one of your subordinates was able to finish her report a day early, you might link it to your own policy of letting her work steadily and independently, with minimal interruptions from you. Or, if you eliminate a meeting, tell your boss how much money the organization saved. Or, mention how instructive you find the time logs that you require periodically from your subordinates—you

had no idea how often you called a certain subordinate on the phone.

WARNING: Of course, the above suggestions imply that your superior is a reasonable individual, amenable to suggestions for improving his or her time management and eager to contribute to the effectiveness of the organization. What if this is not the case? Or, what if you find that you must spend an inordinate amount of time "playing politics" with your boss, flattering him or her, saying yes to proposals or ideas you know are wrong, jockeying for favor?

Alas, there are no simple answers. The only reasonable response is for you to take stock of your objectives, your situation, and your options. At the end of this difficult and painful stocktaking, you might conclude that the price of staying with the organization—under your boss—is too high, and you will begin to look elsewhere for a job. Or, you may conclude that, given the alternatives, you must compromise significantly and stay where you are—for the moment, at least.

How to Deal With a Rush Project From Your Boss

1. *Clarify your superior's instructions.* Find out exactly what the RUSH project entails, what staff you may assign, etc.

2. *Look for short cuts.* If your boss asks for a quick report, Lakein suggests, perhaps a brief report based on information at hand will suffice.

3. *If you oppose doing the project immediately, discuss your objections.* For example, tell your superior that you think what you and your staff are currently working on is more important than the rush project. State your reasons.

4. *Give a realistic estimate of your ability to do the job in the time specified.* Mention relevant factors. Don't promise to meet the deadline if you know it's impossible.

5. *Look for compromises.* Auren Uris gives some useful tips on compromises. He suggests that you can say:

- I can't meet your five o'clock deadline, but I can give you the first section by that time, and the completed project by noon tomorrow. Or,
- My staff can't meet the deadline unless we can get more help from another department. Or,
- I can fill the order only if I do it with regular materials, not with the special formula on the specs.

6. *Motivate your staff.* Explain that the emergency project is top priority, and tell why. Emphasize the challenge, not the burden. Mention whatever rewards your superior has sanctioned: overtime, a bonus, etc.

READ SELECTIVELY...
SPREAD THE LOAD

Problem: Keeping up With the Reading

"Have a nice weekend, Blanche," Vernon Marshall, executive vice president of marketing for Collins Industries, said as he walked to the elevator with his colleague, Blanche Kantner, the company's vice president in charge of research and innovation. "Any special plans?"

Blanche pointed to her bulging briefcase. "Just catch-up reading," she responded. "I can't seem to get around to it during the day. And there's a lot of important new material being published that I have to keep up with."

"Too bad! Hope your husband and kids are understanding."

*   *   *   *   *

Solution: Read Selectively . . .
and Spread the Load

Managers who stuff their briefcases each night or each weekend with professional journals, company reports, long memos, and the latest books in their field can attest to the strain of trying to keep up with the deluge of reading material flooding their desks.

R. Alec Mackenzie indicates the magnitude of the problem. Participants in his time management seminars and lectures report spending 30 percent of their time—*one year in three*—reading.

How to Manage the Flood of Reading

1. *Be selective.* James T. McCay, a time management expert, stresses that it is more important to decide what *not* to read than to be able to read it fast. Thus you can "do away" with a 50,000-word book in one minute if you determine that it is of little use to you.

How to decide if a book is worth reading:

- Scan the table of contents and the cover flaps to determine whether you want to explore the subject now;
- Examine the author's qualifications by reading his or her biography on the cover flaps and checking to see if the bibliography is up to date;

- See if the material is well organized: the table of contents, the preface, and a few chapter-opening paragraphs will reveal this.

Once you've decided that the publication will be useful, how can you find the important information quickly? Again, McCay offers tips:

- Scan the table of contents to get a rough picture of the book's main ideas before you start reading.
- Scan the book quickly—about an hour—to familiarize yourself with the author's thoughts and style. This will help you to understand what the author is saying.
- Carefully read those sections that seem to contain the information you need.

Alan Lakein echoes McCay's advice to read selectively. Applying his favorite prescription for time management, Lakein says it is "more important to read smarter rather than faster."

2. *Delegate reading assignments to your staff.* Ask them to summarize and give you feedback on new developments or ideas highlighted in the reading material. The benefits of delegating reading, according to Mackenzie, include:

- Keeping your staff informed of new developments quickly;
- Spreading reading responsibility fairly;
- Ensuring that printed material is immediately circulated to staff members concerned.

In addition, share with your staff the time-saving tips offered above. And be receptive to your staff's suggestions.

3. *Consider a speed-reading course for yourself and staff members.* But be aware that although a speed-reading course can break bad reading habits, those habits tend to slip back within a few months.

WARNING: Although these techniques will cut down on your reading load, they won't eliminate it. You must still carry your share of the reading burden. In addition, you should skim publications, or portions of them, that a staff member has recommended as having exceptional importance for your organization.

CONCLUSION

Peter Drucker draws an important distinction between efficiency and effectiveness: *Efficiency*, he says, is "the ability to do things right"; *effectiveness* is the "ability to get the right things done." Virtually all time management experts echo this analysis, pointing out its special relevance to today's hard-pressed managers. For managers at all levels, effectiveness is what counts. They must be able to contribute to the major objectives of their organizations; and they can achieve this only by effective planning and rational allocation of resources.

Of all the resources, time is the scarcest—and certainly one of the most vital. Consequently, careful time management is a prime ingredient of managerial effectiveness.

The good news is that effective time management can be learned; the bad news is that it's not easy. For the way you manage your time today is the product of how you handled it five, ten, twenty, thirty years ago. In other words, you have developed certain habits in managing your time; some are good, some bad. But they need not be ingrained. Your goal is to prune the bad habits and substitute good ones in their place.

This substitution takes time, hard work, and patience. You must:

- Become aware of your bad time habits;
- Discard them and substitute productive, time-wise habits; and
- Keep constantly on guard to ward off the sneaky return of the time monsters.

The task is not overwhelming. Gradually, the new, good time habits will become second nature to you, just as your bad ones are now.

Effective time management pays high dividends—for you, your staff, and your organization. Not only does it save time—in the short run and the long—it saves money. Even more important, it saves energy—the physical, mental, and creative energy vital for the well-being of any organization. The choice is between stagnation or growth.

Bibliography

Berkwitt, George J. "The Case of the Fragmented Manager," in *Dun's Review*, April 1969.

Bliss, Edwin C. *Getting Things Done: The ABCs of Time Management*. New York: Charles Scribner's Sons, 1976.

Carlson, Sune. *Executive Behavior: A Study of the Work Load and the Working Methods of Managing Directors*. Stockholm: Stromberg, 1951.

Douglass, Merrill E. *The Time Management Workbook*. Grandville, Michigan: Time Management Center, 1979.

Drucker, Peter F. *The Effective Executive*. New York: Harper & Row, 1967.

Lakein, Alan. *How to Get Control of Your Life and Your Time*. New York: Signet, 1974.

Mackenzie, R. Alec. *The Time Trap*. New York: McGraw-Hill Paperback, 1975.

Mackenzie, R. Alec and Lekan, Dennis. "Take a 'Quiet Hour' . . . for Time to Think and Plan," in *The Time Management Workbook*, by Merrill E. Douglass, *op. cit.*

McCay, James T. *The Management of Time*. Englewood Cliffs, N.J.: Prentice-Hall, 1959.

Reynolds, Helen and Tramel, Mary E. *Executive Time Management*. Englewood Cliffs, N.J.: Prentice-Hall, 1979.

Schwartz, Eleanor B. and Mackenzie, R. Alec. "Time-Management Strategy for Women," in *Management Review*. New York: AMACOM, 1977.

Uris, Auren. *The Executive Deskbook*. 2nd ed. New York: Van Nostrand Reinhold Company, 1976.

Webber, Ross A. *Time and Management*. New York: Van Nostrand Reinhold Co., 1972.